SONG IN THE WILDERNESS

Salem College Edition

1772-1947

___Paul Green___

___Charles Vardell___

COPY NUMBER 339

A Salem Composition of an Earlier Day.

Song in the Wilderness

CANTATA FOR CHORUS AND ORCHESTRA

with Baritone Solo

Poem

By Paul Green

Music

By Charles Vardell

The University of North Carolina Press

Chapel Hill

1947

COPYRIGHT, 1947
BY
THE UNIVERSITY OF NORTH CAROLINA PRESS

First edition, limited to six hundred numbered copies
autographed by the author and the composer.

*Designed, Printed and Bound by the Offset Lithography Division
of
Independent Music Publishers, New York City*

DEDICATED

To the enduring memory of the pioneers of Wachovia, whose hands builded in the wilderness a house of peace and brotherhood; whose eyes were lifted to the distant horizons of the spirit; and who cherished in their sturdy hearts the precious and honorable gift of song.

COMMITTEE ON PLANS

175th Anniversary
Salem College

Mrs. Henry Alvah Strong,
    Honorary Chairman
Dr. Agnew H. Bahnson, *Chairman*
Dr. Walser Allen
Dr. Adelaide Fries
Mr. Gordon Gray
Miss Mary Hunter Hackney
Mr. Ralph P. Hanes

Mrs. T. Holt Haywood
Mrs. C. T. Leinbach
Dr. N. R. McEwen
Dr. Howard E. Rondthaler
Mr. Pen Sandridge
Mrs. R. D. Shore
Dr. C. G. Vardell, Jr.
Mrs. Henry Voges

Foreword

Love of God and of liberty! What a power these things were in the settlement of our country! From Massachusetts to California there was perhaps no state that did not have its bands of settlers who, being associated together by common ideologies and common purposes, went to unsettled regions and there built homes, churches, and schools. They usually perhaps thought of themselves as doing nothing heroic or singular. They were only bringing their families and their household goods to a new land which they no doubt hoped to make by hard labor and much privation as much like the lands they had left as they possibly could. They also brought their neighbors and were glad to do so. It is difficult to think of the now rich and settled state of North Carolina as having had many of these groups (usually united by religious ties) come into its then sparsely occupied hills and valleys. Taking the country as a whole, the differences of creed and custom seemed to the newcomers themselves no doubt irreconcilable, perhaps in some cases they still seem so; but in spite of that they present a common pattern and texture varied in detail mainly as a weaver or a painter sprinkles charming variety over a field of unity.

Many of the communities thus formed left written records usually of vital matters —births, marriages, and deaths—and also of the purchase of land, the election of officials, the building of schools and churches, and the establishment of new subsidiary settlements. The settlers seem usually to have been plain, perhaps indifferently educated people, and yet in almost every case these pioneer communities had in their midst, and usually as their leaders, men and women of education and culture.

These people produced few books no doubt, but good letters and good journals were plentiful. It has, for the most part, been left to the loving and painstaking labor of later generations, often of lineal descendants, to tell the story and interpret the spirit of these bands of pioneer Christians, who were not so much engaged in the interpretation of themselves as engaged face to face with the problems presented by labor, hardships, and poverty — just living — while at the same time they were founding civil and religious institutions in the new land. In our region of the country we have considerable numbers of sometimes quite recent books which endeavor to reveal the minds and hearts of these silent people of an earlier day so fully that, were they living, they might say, "Were we really like that?" And in simple modesty they might be able to answer, "I hope we were." They would be proud of having once been such men and women. One thinks of Adelaide Fries's *The Road to Salem*, Dorothy Gilbert's *Guilford: A Quaker College*, Gerald White Johnson's *By Reason of Strength*. There are doubtless many other books which try to make the past live.

But the heart demands a record made by a poet, who knows and feels the beauty of the land, the trees (not yet cut down), the rivers, and the clouds; who is able also to restore to life the finer spirit of aspiration and the deeper urge of sincere living. In his poem Paul Green, appropriately the author of *The Lost Colony*, has given us the finer spirit, not only of the ancestors of many men and women of North Carolina, but also of the ancestors of many native Americans throughout the whole republic. Poetry has done this, and Charles Vardell has brought his imagination and his distinguished skill to the translation of emotions, ideas, and aspirations into music.

In the presence of this little work sectional differences tend to disappear, and the pious spirit of our ancestors appears again. California skies are not unlike these, and Kentucky woods as they flourish (alas! mainly in our memories) are the same as these. And I am sure the hearts of Californians and Kentuckians, as well as North Carolinians, respond to these old emotions and ambitions and seek to keep them within the scope of revival and recall.

It has been my lot to know and assist many young Americans who, like the pioneers, brought to the task of their own educations nothing but aspiration, willingness to work, and simple faith in God. We think of these modern pioneers as we contemplate this work; we wave our hands to these survivors of a bygone time and wish them Godspeed.

One hundred and seventy-five years is a long time in our land, and in the work before us we pay respectful honor to Salem College as both old in service and vigorous in its perennial youth.

University of North Carolina   HARDIN CRAIG

SONG IN THE WILDERNESS

SONG IN THE WILDERNESS

1.

Here in the heart of these deep woods,
In the peace and bosomed richness of these hills,
Our forefathers came seeking a dwelling place,
A shelter for themselves and the light they cherished.
Not by hate and the iron fist, they said,
But by love and the friendly open hand
Shall a man survive the greenery of his days
And reap the mellow harvest of his soul.
Here upon this very spot, this sacred place, they stood
And set their living credo up, a faith,
Like a tree to flourish by the waterside!

2.

Treading the dolorous way,
From lands afar they came—
Through heat and snow and burning sleet.
The wind and weather, treachery and flood,
The wheel and lash, the garrote and the screw
They suffered!
Poor frail and tottering forms,
Oh weak and shuddering hands uplifted!
Still with their last breath, with their last motion
Proclaiming the vision affirmative!—
The broken bones of those who died,
The piteous splintered tongues of martyrs
Strewing the way of woe and death.—
Signs and talismans multitudinous
Of the truth that lived the more they died!

3.

And the marching feet kept marching—
Out of the wastelands, out of their desolation,
Over the flints and shards of pain,
Across the fens and mires,
Up the rivers,
Through the waters tumultuous,
Gathering, moving,
Towards the western sun,
Bright and glowing orb in the sky,
Symbol of the flame burning in their hearts,
Quenchless and eternal,
Symbol of the truth made manifest,
That sinks to rise an ever-recurrent dawn
In the will and faith of righteous men—
Marching, moving on
Toward a land of freedom,
Toward the abiding place of the spirit!

4.

And on a blessed morning they arrived.
And the earth was good.
The trees are taller here, they said,
Tougher and harder-grained for building.
Here the grass is greener,
The stone more abundant and available to our hand,
The waters fresher, the winds sweeter,
The birds of the air more melodious.
Verily the Lord hath smiled upon this land
And sanctified it for our habitation.
Here our hurt limbs may be healed,
Our sorrows eased and our tears be dried away.
Call forth the cherished organ, incased and protected,
Throw back the covers, open it wide,
Pull out the stops untrammeled.
Let the jubilate sound abroad,
The prophetic word echo in the hills,
The horns ring out their glad tidings!
Sleepers awaken!
The green leaves of the trees themselves
Shall shake their congratulation,
The birds carry our praise and thanksgiving aloft
Into the wakeless reaches of the sky.

5.

Dig, dig, dig,
Chop, chop, chop,
The pick and mattock and spade,
The hammer and axe and saw!—
The slip and slide of the shaving plane,
The sharp metallic ring of the mason's trowel
In the frosty upland morning—
A symphony of sound, of energy,
A song creative, vibrant in harmony—
The trees offering their stout hearts,
Majestic timbers uprearing,
The durable stone itself yielding its stiff will,
The cement and mortar and the clay cooperating,
Fusing and mixing in a blessed enterprise,
The group and cause and common glory of all—
To build a dwelling-place in the wilderness,
To build a tabernacle for brotherhood,
The unity that beats from heart to heart,
Unitas Fratrum—
Love abiding!

6.

Oh let us arise and with adequate words pour out
A statement all-powerful, all-thundering,
Strong in its drive, surging with inspiration,
Worthy of our forefathers and the truth they served!
There is nothing greater than what they did here,
Nothing more requiring our devotion and our praise,
Nothing to be imagined of wider reach,
Of more challenging significance.
Let us think upon it, ponder it well,
Let it sink into the inmost recesses of our heart.
Remember, oh, let us remember!—
Faith of our fathers, the truth they followed,
Rising spontaneous, springing within us!

7.

This is the accepted hour then, and this the place.
Let us lift our voices in proud affirmation,
Singing their song again as they sang it before us.
Let us cry the diapason of our beliefs aloud,
Let us be heard—
Here within the valleys of evening,
Here among the hills of morning,
Here among these trees and ancient buildings,
Hearth and home of their ever-living faith—
Love, unity, brotherhood, peace,
Peace, brotherhood, unity, love—
That we may escape confusion and darkness,
The waste and woe and blindness unutterable!—
Let the refrain resounding pass through the doors,
Into the open spaces, over the fields,
Through the cities and into the byways!
Sing, sing, loudly proclaim it,
Tireless and unremitting until it is heard,
Until it is heeded!
Sing the ideal triumphant, the message eternal,
That we may live!—
From this spot, this place consecrated,
Peace among men,
That we may be blessed!
Amen.
Love among men,
Lest we perish!
Amen! Amen!

—PAUL GREEN

INSTRUMENTATION

One Flute
Two Oboes
Two Clarinets in B Flat
Two Bassoons
Two Horns in F
Two Trumpets in B Flat
One Tenor Trombone
Timpani
Percussion
Piano
Strings

Orchestral score and parts of this cantata may be rented upon application to the composer, Charles G. Vardell, Jr., Salem College, Winston-Salem, N. C.

SONG IN THE WILDERNESS

CANTATA FOR CHORUS AND ORCHESTRA
with Baritone Solo

Poem by Paul Green

Music by Charles Vardell

12

II Andante quasi adagio

32

34

36

38

40

42

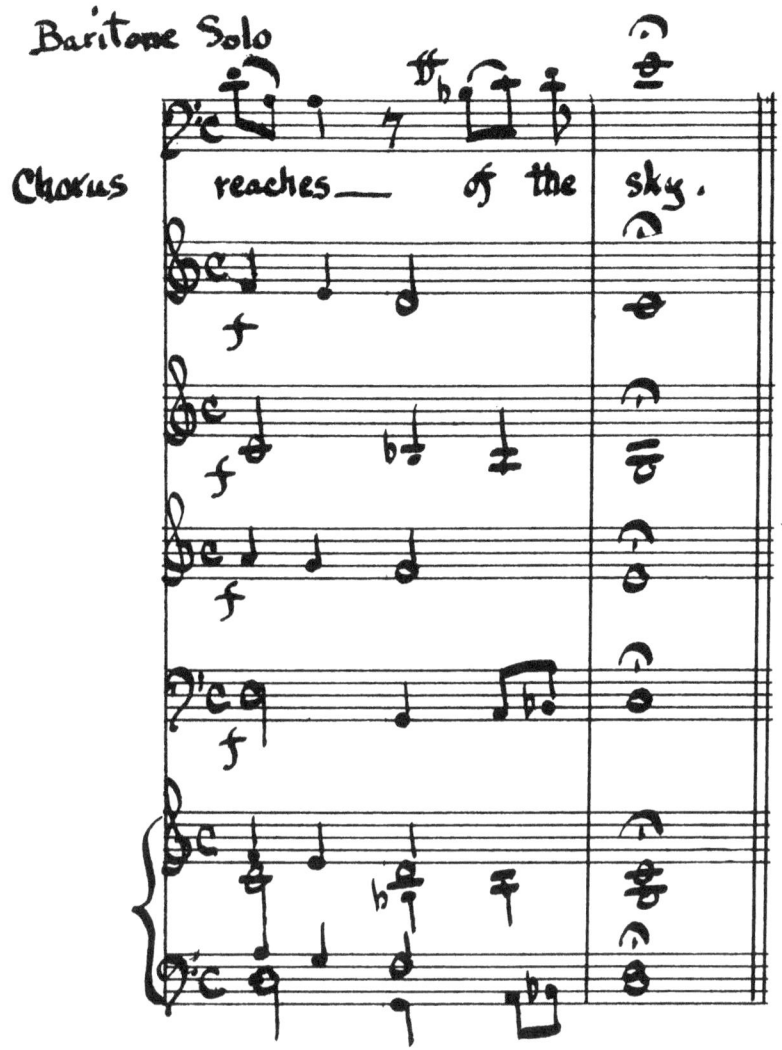

44

VI Allegro moderato e marcato

48

65

Baritone Solo

76

Chorus

78

Baritone Solo

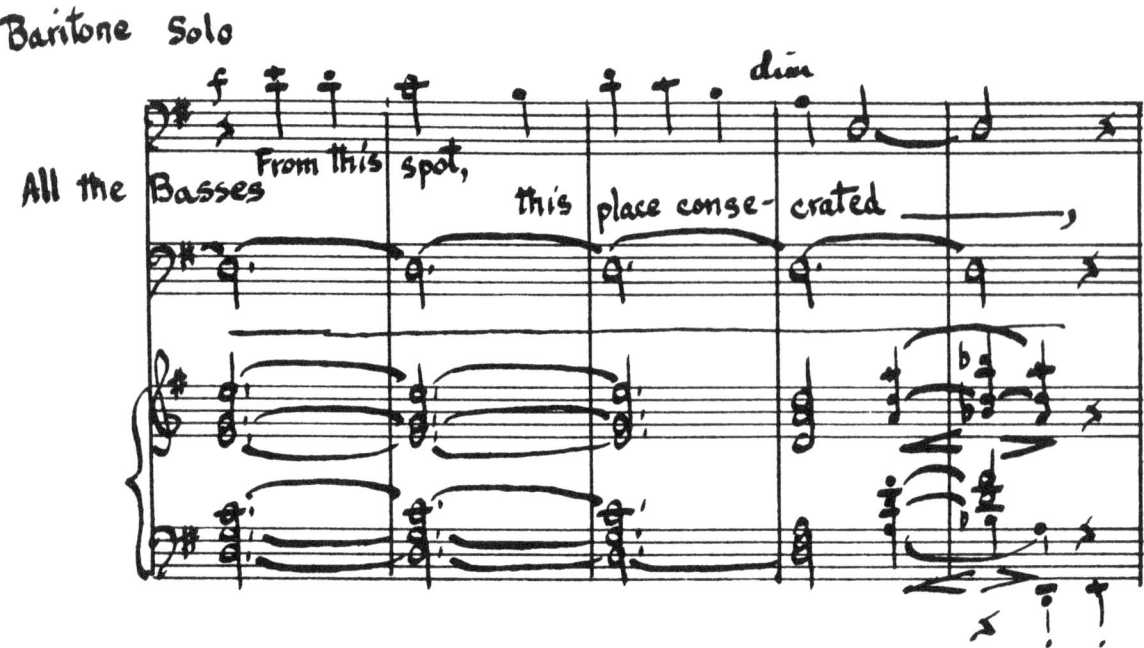

All the Basses: From this spot, this place conse- crated

Full Chorus

Love among men

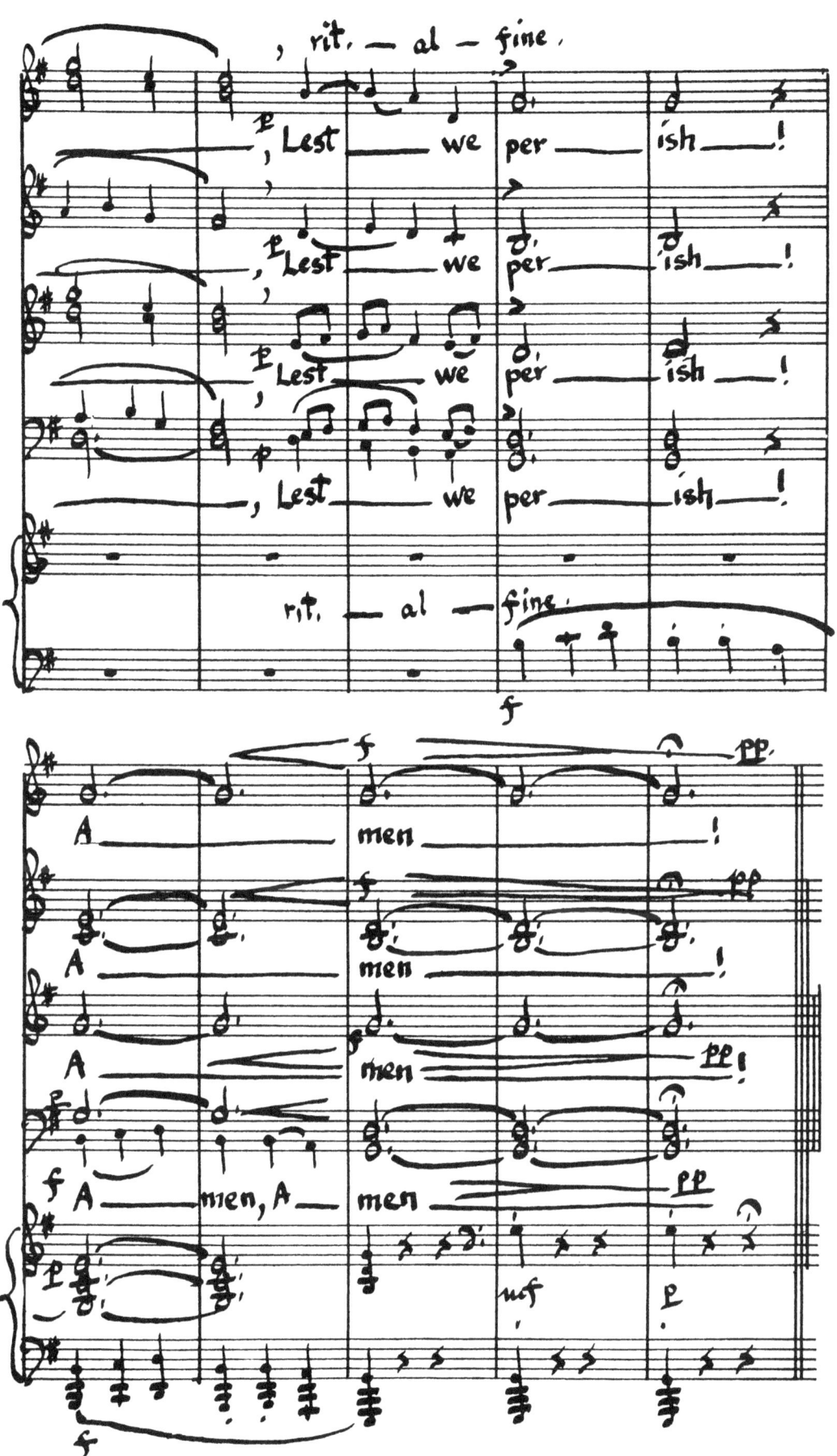

www.ingramcontent.com/pod-product-compliance
Lightning Source LLC
Chambersburg PA
CBHW081423230426
43668CB00016B/2330